First Birthday

by Linda Valentino

Celebrate birthday memories with a great collection of toys, colored papers, balloons and happy photos.

SIZE: 8" x 10"

MATERIALS:
Shadowbox 8" x 10" Brown frame with hinges • Birthday photos • Balloon image • Papers (Blue gingham, Yellow stars, Yellow stripes, Red stripes) • Red cardstock • Multi-colored paper basket fill • 7 miniature toys • White letter stickers $1\frac{1}{4}$" • Happy Birthday sticker • Double-sided tape • 3D foam dots • Tacky glue

INSTRUCTIONS:
Tape Blue paper to backing. Mat photos with Red and Yellow papers. Adhere photos to background. Cut a $4\frac{1}{4}$" tall number from Yellow paper. Cut 3 Red numbers $4\frac{3}{8}$" tall. Mat the Yellow on a Red and use 3D dots to adhere the remaining Red ones. Tape to bottom left of frame. Cut out balloon image and adhere with 2 sets of 3D dots. Adhere birthday token to page. Glue several toys and basket fill to bottom of shadowbox. Close box and apply name stickers to the frame.

Adhere ribbons on top and on the sides.

Adhere ribbons at an angle on the top of the box.

Ribbon Covered Mini Box

photo on page 2

Dive into your ribbon stash and have fun!

SIZE: $2\frac{5}{8}$" x $2\frac{5}{8}$" x 2" tall

MATERIALS:
Wood Box $2\frac{5}{8}$" x $2\frac{5}{8}$" x 2" • Photo cropped to 2" x 2" • 1 yard (2 ribbons $\frac{5}{8}$" wide, 2 ribbons $\frac{3}{8}$" wide) • *Xyron* sticker maker • Scissors • Craft knife

INSTRUCTIONS:
Cut ribbon pieces to fit the box, allowing $\frac{1}{2}$" overlap. Run the ribbons through the sticker maker. Cover the bottom of the box with ribbons adhering the overlap evenly up both sides. Then cover the top of the box, adding ribbons on a diagonal last. • Trim the ribbon away from the hinges. • Place a 2" x 2" photo in the shadowbox.

Tiled Mini Box

photo on page 2

MATERIALS:
Wood Box • $\frac{3}{8}$" x $\frac{3}{8}$" mosaic tiles • White grout • Tacky glue

INSTRUCTIONS:
Position tiles as desired (allow space for hinges and clasp). Glue tiles one at a time. Let dry. • Protect glass with painter's tape. • Mix grout, press between tiles and smooth with your fingers. Keep grout away from the hinges and lid. Let grout set for a few minutes. Sponge away excess grout from the top of tiles. Let grout set overnight. Polish tiles with a soft cloth.

Glue tiles in place, then add grout.

Soldier's Creed

by Michele Charles

Honor the sacrifices of every guardian of freedom with a recognition of duty, discipline, and service.

SIZE: 12" x 12"

MATERIALS:
Shadowbox frame 12" x 12" • Photo • Medals • Bars • Photo paper • Black foam core board • Computer • Scanner • Craft knife • Adhesive • Hot glue gun

INSTRUCTIONS:
Scan medals and bars and enlarge photo. Print onto photo paper. • Print "25 Years of Service" banner on photo paper and print "Soldier's Creed". • Cut out images and adhere to foam core board. Cut out with craft knife. • Adhere elements to back panel. Reassemble shadowbox frame.

Basic Steps for a Dimensional Photo:
1. Adhere images to foam core board and cut out.
2. Use hot glue to adhere soldier to inside of shadowbox frame.

The Soldier's Creed

I am an American Soldier.

I am a Warrior and a member of a team. I serve the people of the United States and live the Army Values.

I will always place the mission first.

I will never accept defeat.

I will never quit.

I will never leave a fallen comrade.

I am disciplined, physically and mentally tough, trained and proficient in my warrior tasks and drills. I always maintain my arms, equipment, and myself.

I am an expert and I am a professional.

I stand ready to deploy, engage, and destroy the enemies of the United States of America in close combat.

I am a guardian of freedom and the American way of life.

I am an American Soldier.

Sailor

by Linda Valentino

Anchors Aweigh! Preserve the memory and tell the story of your family's military service.

SIZE: 12" x 12"

MATERIALS:

Shadowbox 12" x 12" • Military photos • Dog tag and medals • Flag paper • Cardstock (Blue, White) • *K&Company* Navy foil embossed stickers • Ribbons (Four 13" Red ¼" wide, 13" White ⅝" wide) • 2 White straight pins • Computer and printer • Double-sided tape • Fabric glue • 3D foam dots

INSTRUCTIONS:

Cut flag paper to fit in box, adhere in place. Glue ribbons to the frame. Let dry. Pin metals to White ribbon. Mat photos and adhere to background. Print label with name, date and age. Mat and adhere to bottom of photo. Pin dog tag down left side. Apply Navy stickers to page. Close frame. Adhere 3 star stickers.

Tips for Freestanding Photos

Choose a person in the photograph that is posed in an interesting way. If a certain position is needed, pose a person and take a new shot.

Using the original photo or a copy of the photo, carefully cut around the person. Make an even better dimensional photo by adhering the photo to a piece of foam core (Black is best). Then cut around the photo with a craft knife.

Stick 3D foam dots to several places on the back of the cutout. Press in place.

Make a Dimensional Photo:
1. Adhere image to foam core.

2. Cut out image.

Hornets Team

by Michele Charles

Before the moths eat into that old letter jacket, preserve it in a shadowbox. It's a wonderful way to show off those championship patches.

SIZE: 12" x 12"

MATERIALS:

Shadowbox frame 12" x 12" • Letter jacket • Patches • Sports photo • Black foam core board • Computer • Scanner • Photo paper • Gray spray paint • Craft knife • Adhesive • Hot glue gun

INSTRUCTIONS:

Spray paint shadowbox frame. Let dry. • Scan sports patches. Reduce and print onto photo paper. Cut out images. • Adhere photo, letter "G" and state patch to foam core board. Cut out. • Arrange sports memorabilia in shadowbox. • Adhere patches and patch printouts to back panel. Glue foot of sports player to inside base of shadowbox frame. Reassemble frame.

Wedding

by Linda Valentino

Enhance wedding photos and capture the sentiment of the day.

SIZE: 10" x 10"

MATERIALS:

Shadowbox 10" x 10" Cream frame with hinges • Wedding photos • Cream ½" wide ribbon (two 11", three 10") • Cardstock (White, Black, Cream) • 2 ⅜" buttons • 3 pearl head pins • 6" x 28" White tulle • 6 Cream silk flowers • 15" Gold 22 gauge wire • ¼" Pearl beads to make 11" chain • Decorative edged scissors • Computer and printer • Double-sided tape • Fabric glue • 3D foam dots

INSTRUCTIONS:

Glue two 11" ribbons to frame down center 1" apart. Let dry. • Glue 10" ribbons to backing 1½" from sides. • Mat main photo on layers of cardstock: photo-White-Black-Cream. Trim Cream cardstock with decorative scissors. Make a bow from 10" piece of ribbon, trim, and glue to top of photo. Glue to center ribbons. • Mat 3 smaller photos on White cardstock and adhere to background ribbons. Print names and date on White cardstock, mat with Black cardstock, and glue between photos. Adhere buttons and flower in place. Crinkle tulle along bottom of box and glue in place. Thread pearls on wire to make 11" chain. Wrap ends to secure. Coil slightly and pin. Glue 2 flowers on left and 3 on right hiding pins.

Sister Shadowbox

by Paula Phillips

Absolutely elegant! The ribbon colors and mats complement the photos perfectly.

SIZE: 10" x 10"

MATERIALS:

Shadowbox 10" x 10" hinged • Blue cardstock • Ribbons (1 yd 1½" wide plaid, 3 yds ¼" wide Lavender) • 12" Blue ⅜" wide rickrack • 1 yd. pearl trim • 25 Satin rose buds • Silk flowers (Blue, Lavender) • 10 pearl head pins • 2 small wood shapes • 5 small pearls • 1 medium glue dot • Tacky tape

INSTRUCTIONS:

Tape Lavender ribbon around the outside of the frame. Cut 4 pieces of Plaid ribbon for the corners and adhere in place. • Tape rickrack to background. Mat photos and adhere to background. Tape ribbon around photos creating a frame. Add pearl pins to photo corners and rickrack. • Tape ribbon to the back of both wood shapes and attach the ribbon to the shadowbox allowing the pieces to hang. • Adhere loose pearls to center of flower. Adhere to background.

Flower Bouquet: Thread each rosebud onto a pearl head pin, then pin in place. Weave pearl trim around the roses leaving some loops showing. Use additional pearl head pins to hold the trim in place. Pin silk flowers into the gaps.

Making the Sister Shadowbox

1. Adhere the ribbon to the photo.

2. Pin the flowers to the backboard.

3. Tape the Lavender ribbon to the top of the box.

4. Adhere the Plaid ribbon to corners.

Dance

by Linda Valentino

Create a memory as beautiful as the Dance. Sparkling rhinestones and hanging slippers create an unmistakable theme in this pretty pink frame.

SIZE: 12" x 12"

MATERIALS:
Shadowbox 12" x 12" unpainted wooden frame • Dance photos • Flowered & gingham paper • Cardstock: (White, Black, Pink, Dark Pink) • Ballet slippers • 5mm rhinestones (6 Lavender, 5 Pink, 5 Yellow) • Pink ribbon (12" sheer 5/8" wide, 9" Gingham 3/8" wide, four 5" assorted 1/4" wide for tying around the letter) • *Simply Stamps* Jive Alphabet foam letter "O"• 3" White wooden letters • *DecoArt* Americana acrylics (Baby Pink, Pink Chiffon, White Wash) • *FM Brush Co.* Dynasty paintbrush • Double-sided tape • Thick tacky glue • 3D foam dots

INSTRUCTIONS:
Paint frame White Wash and inside frame Pink Chiffon. Let dry. Apply Pink Chiffon paint to foam stamp and stamp around White frame. Repeat with Baby Pink. • Cut flowered and gingham papers to fit inside frame. Adhere sheer ribbon over the seam, turning the ends to the back of the page. Tape paper inside frame. • Cover the letter D with flowered paper and knot short ribbons around the letter. Mat photos and adhere to frame. Glue rhinestones to corners of photo mats, letters and background. • Glue strings of ballet slippers down center. Make a bow with Gingham ribbon and glue at top of slipper strings. • Stand up frame and glue wooden letters to bottom. Let dry.

SIZE: 12" x 12"

MATERIALS:
Shadowbox 12" x 12" hinged • Decorative paper • 2" x 3" White and Aqua cardstock for journal box • Clock face • Brass clock hands • Brad • Die cuts (computer, van, baby items, sunflower) • Small bunny • Drawing figure • $1 dollar bill • 4" x4" fabric for apron • Alpha Rub-ons • Rub-on Stitching Curly Q • Hot glue • Foam Pop Dots

INSTRUCTIONS:
Trim paper to fit inside box.
Apron: Cut two 2" x 4" fabric rectangles. Use pattern to cut one fabric piece for apron top. Pin top to the fabric rectangle in center. Sew the two pieces together. At the top of the apron, sew a long Running stitch and gather. Use Pop Dots to attach to figure. Glue a sunflower to apron skirt.
Finish: Adhere clock face, hands and brad to background paper. Accordion fold $ bill and glue to figure's hand. • Hot glue bunny to background. • Copy journaling onto cardstock, cut and layer. Adhere remaining objects. • Clean glass & apply rub-ons to outside front on glass.

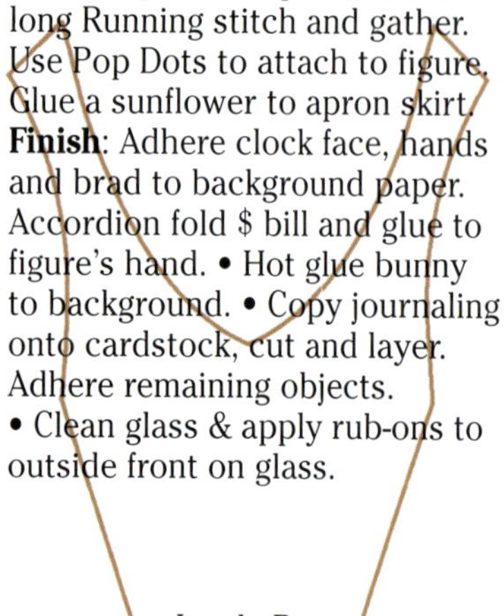

Juggle Box
Apron Top

Juggle Box

by Cyndi Hansen

Pay tribute to all the tasks a busy mom handles in the course of every day with this delightful shadowbox, so appropriately named.

Wineries

by Linda Valentino

Unique travels create wonderful memories. Preserving the moments in a shadowbox allows you to display the wonderful collectibles from your trip.

SIZE: 8" x 10" x 2" deep

MATERIALS:
Shadowbox 8" x 10" x 2" • Cardstock (Medium Green, Dark Green, Violet) • Artificial grapes • 15 Wine corks • Round metal self-adhesive letters to spell "WINERIES' • 4 Brown eyelets • 3 straight pins • Winery photos • Wine bottle image • Eyelet tools • Thick tacky glue • Double-sided tape • 3D foam dots

INSTRUCTIONS:
Remove backing from frame. Glue 11 corks to bottom inside of frame and 3 corks to top of frame. Cut out wine bottle image and stick between corks on right side. Let dry. • On backing, pin grapes down left side. Mat photos and set eyelets in corners. Apply metal letters. Adhere photos to backing. Glue one cork above top photo. Let dry. Reassemble frame.

'Sing' Shadowbox

by Cyndi Hansen

If feathered friends make your heart sing, create this simple display for your favorite room. The bird image comes from an old greeting card.

SIZE: 9" x 11" x 2½" deep

MATERIALS:
Shadowbox 9" x 11" • Bird image • Decorative papers • Twig • Silk flowers • Nest • Small plastic eggs • White chipboard letters • Opalescent embossing powder • Embossing ink • Diluted White acrylic paint • Paintbrush • Hot glue • Double-sided tape • Foam tape

INSTRUCTIONS:
Cover backboard with decorative papers. Drybrush White paint around the edge of the bird image and the background papers. Let dry. • Emboss chipboard letters with Opalescent powder. • Adhere bird image and letters to backboard. Glue nest, twigs, and flowers to the inside of the frame. Reassemble shadowbox.

Old Photos

by Cyndi Hansen

"Grandpa, do you remember when you took me camping at Lake Cayuga? We had so much fun." Preserve those special memories in a shadowbox frame with coordinating natural accents.

SIZE: 9" x 20"

MATERIALS:
Shadowbox 9" x 20" • *Die Cuts with a View* Printable Transparency sheet • Decorative papers (*Cosmo Cricket, We R Memory Keepers*) • *Design Originals* mini clips • *K&Company* (tags, stickers) • Naturals acorns and leaves • Rubber stamps (Number, alphabet) • *Ranger* Brown inkpad • *AMACO* stamp pad for metal • Foam Pop dots

INSTRUCTIONS:
Cut decorative paper strips in different widths and arrange on shadowbox backboard. Lightly tape together on back of papers. Sew a Running stitch or Zigzag stitch. Adhere stitched paper to backboard and trim as needed. • Mat photos, ink the edges, and adhere to background. Apply sticker sayings. Ink clips and let dry. Clip naturals and tag to photos. • Stamp words and date, tear out, and adhere to background with Pop Dots. • Use botanical pattern of choice to copy onto transparency. Cut transparency in half lengthwise. • Place transparency on glass, cut to fit, and glue along edge.

1. Sew randomly over the decorative papers.

2. Cut out the card.

3. Wrap the fibers and rounder punch the corners.

4. Adhere the photo with glue dots.

'Elephant Safari' Shadowbox

by Cyndi Hansen

Display images of your favorite animals in a frame.

SIZE: 9" x 20"

MATERIALS:

Shadowbox 9" x 20" • Photos • Decorative papers • Cardstock • Reeds • Metal charm • Fibers • Beads • Chipboard letters • Black foam core board • 2 tiny cup hooks • Black marker • Black wire • Corner rounder punch • Deckle edge scissors • Craft knife • Sanding block • Craft glue • Pop dots

INSTRUCTIONS:

Cover backboard with decorative papers.

Cards: Tear papers and layer on cardstock. Sew swirls and lines randomly over paper. Cut paper into 5 cards 2½" x 3½". Use corner rounder punch on each corner. Add fibers, beads, and charms. Mat small photos and trim mat with deckle scissors. Adhere to card with Pop Dots. • Tear a handmade paper slightly larger than the card and adhere to card. Glue to backboard. • Choose 3 reeds to lie on top of paper strip. Cut a long length of fiber, loosely wind around reeds and tie off. String beads on each end of fiber and tie off. Cut paper strip to fit and glue strip and reeds to board. Tear a small paper square and glue to center of reeds and then glue a charm on top.

Sign: Go around edges of each chipboard letter with Black marker. Cover letters with decorative paper and smooth edges with a sanding block. Cut foam core board to fit word. Smooth edges of foam core with sanding block. Adhere decorative paper and letters to foam core. • Use an awl to poke a hole thru foam core 2" from each end. Run a long piece of Black wire thru each hole. At top edge bend wire over to create a loop and then wrap wire around. For bottom, wrap wire around reed a couple of times then back up and around top to secure. Repeat for other side. • Screw small cup hooks into bottom of frame to hang sign. Use a Black marker to color the hooks and then add a reed on top.

'Huff' Family Shadowbox

by Paula Phillips

Create gorgeous home decor with a family history shadowbox. The fence, wagon wheel and boots at the bottom give this box character and a feeling of the old west.

SIZE: 12" x 12"

MATERIALS:
Shadowbox 12" x 12" x 1 3/8" • 2 sticks of unfinished molding • Decorative 2" wood squares • 12" x 12" papers (2 Dark Brown, 1 Light Tan, 1 Olive Green, 1 printed) • Wood & wire miniature fence • (Miniature wagon wheel, Western ornaments) • Small piece of greenery • 8" White crocheted lace • 12 small brads • Chipboard alphabet • Twine • Ink pads (Dark Brown, Olive Green) • Mod Podge • Wood stain • 2 Foam brushes • Sandpaper • Old towel or rag • Craft knife • 1/16" hole punch • Tacky glue • Wood glue • Medium Glue Dots • Pop Dots • Double-sided tape

INSTRUCTIONS:
Cut molding to fit frame. Sand the edges of the trim and lightly sand the unfinished shadowbox. • Following manufacturer's instructions, apply stain to wood pieces and shadowbox. Wipe off the excess stain with the rag. Let dry.
• Adhere trim and squares with wood glue. • Cover the background with paper. Cut 4 Green strips of Green 1/4" wide and adhere around edge of page.
• Tint the crocheted trim with Brown inkpad and adhere to page. Tape background paper to shadowbox. Mat photos with Brown and Olive Green paper. Cut Brown triangles for photo corners and adhere in place. Ink the edges of photo mats with Dark Brown and tape in place.
• Cover chipboard letters with Dark Brown paper using Mod Podge. Punch holes in the letters and add brads. Ink the edges of the letters with Olive Green and adhere to page. • Glue the greenery, wagon wheel, fence, hat, and boots in place. Wrap the twine around 2 fingers three times to make a lasso and adhere it to a fence slat.

1. Stain the trim.

2. Glue trim to frame.

Seashell Box

by Cyndi Hansen

Andre Gide, a French philosopher, wrote "Man cannot discover new oceans until he has the courage to lose sight of the shore." Shadowboxes give us an opportunity to express in tangible form the philosophies we hold most dear.

SIZE: 10" x 10"

MATERIALS:
Shadowbox 10" x 10" • Decorative papers • *Cosmo Cricket* (Border stickers, Chipboard letters) • Seashells • Black foam core board • White stamp pad • White embossing powder • Heat gun • Deckle edge scissors • Craft glue • Pop Dots • Large glue dots

INSTRUCTIONS:
Measure inside of box and cut foam core pieces following the diagram. Cut notches so they fit together. Place inside of box to verify the fit. Remove foam core, cut background papers and adhere to back of foam core. Let dry. Adhere this piece to backboard. • Cover edges of foam core with sticker borders. • Print quote on cardstock and cut out with deckle edge scissors. Stamp the front of each letter with ink and sprinkle with embossing powder. • Adhere shells, starfish, letters, and quote in place. • Assemble frame and adhere borders to the front of the box.

We cannot discover
new oceans until we have
the courage to lose sight
of the shore.

–Gide

Foam core pieces front view diagram.

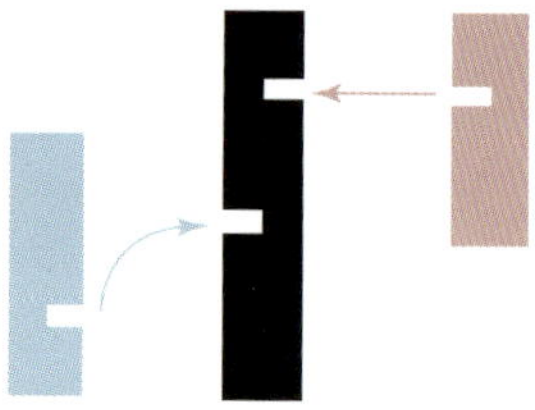

Foam core pieces side view with notches.

Tip:
Make sure notches are cut so pieces fit tight - start small and cut larger a bit at a time.

Happiness Shadowbox

by Cyndi Hansen

"Happiness is something that comes into our lives through a door we don't remember leaving open." Invite the serenity of the forest into your home with a shadowbox that preserves a bit of nature.

SIZE: 14" x 14"

MATERIALS:
Shadowbox 14" x 14" • Papers (Handmade, Decorative) • 3 rocks • Dried leaves • Twigs • Acorns • 2 decorative brads • Foam stamp • Blue acrylic paint • Chalk • Foam dots • Hot glue

INSTRUCTIONS:
Cover backboard with decorative paper. Randomly stamp leaves with Blue paint. Let dry. • Tear handmade paper into 2 strips, adhering 1 vertically and one horizontally on background. Glue rocks and twigs in place. • Print quote, tear out and highlight with chalk. Glue to decorative paper and attach brads. Adhere to background with foam dots.

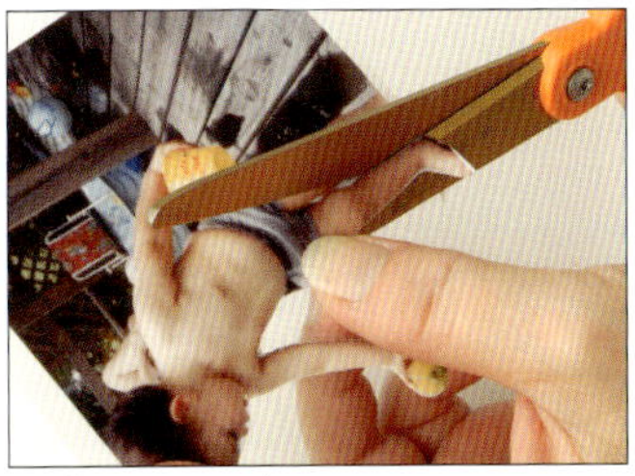

1. Cut out photos.

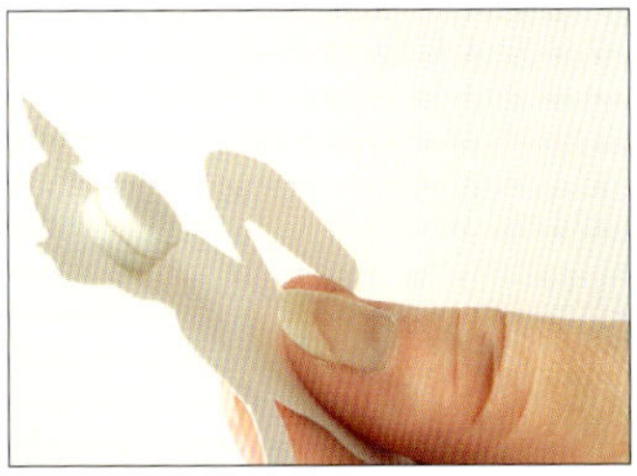

2. Stack glue dots on the back.

Beach Photo Scene

by Linda Valentino

Capture the depth and dimension of a scene with this fun diorama technique.

SIZE: 6½" x 7"

MATERIALS:
Shadowbox 6½" x 7" • Photos • Decorative paper • *Provo Craft* 4" wood sun • 30 small seashells • *DecoArt* Americana Mink Tan acrylic paint • *FM Brush Co.* Dynasty paintbrush • Tacky glue • 3D foam dots • Glue dots

INSTRUCTIONS:
Paint frame inside and out with Mink Tan. Enlarge ocean photo or use a scrapbook paper cut to fit backing. Cut around 2 children and adhere to ocean backing using one or 2 sets of 3D dots. Use glue dots to press small shells in hands or pails of children. Glue shells to bottom of shadowbox. Let dry. Reassemble frame. Glue sun to top of frame.

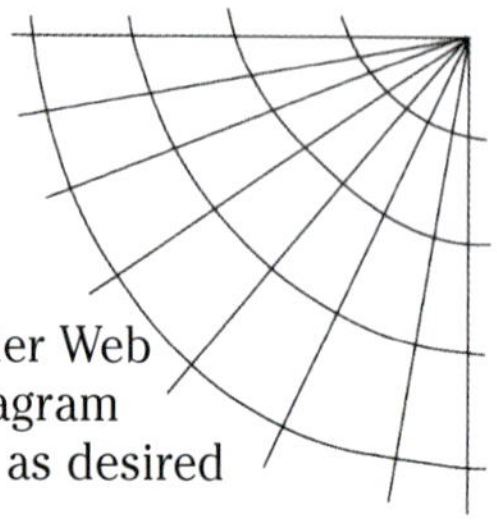

Spider Web
Diagram
Enlarge as desired

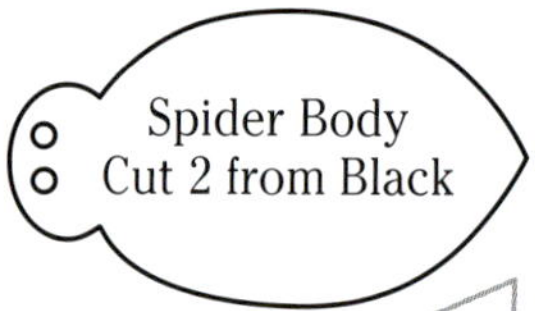

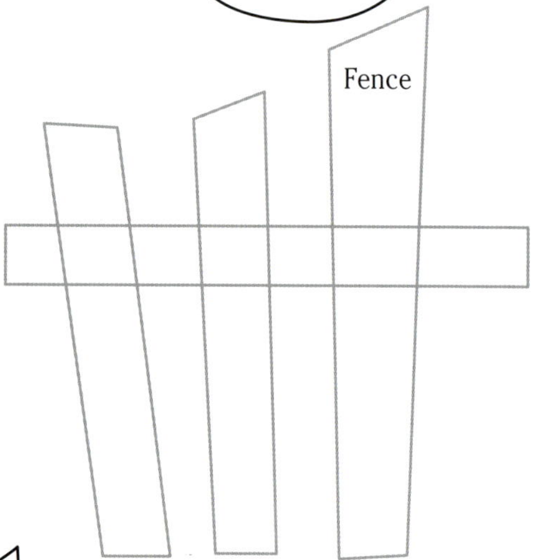

Halloween Box

by Cyndi Hansen

Craft spooky decor brimming with Halloween fun.

SIZE: 14" x 14"

MATERIALS:

Shadowbox 14" x 14" • Orange paper • Cardstock (Yellow, Black, Orange, Gray) • Moss • Small rocks • Ornamental tree • Batting • Black wire • Clear fishing line • Black pen • White colored pencil • Decorative chalk • White paint • Skeleton stencil • Foam Pop dots • Craft glue • Hot glue • Glue gun • Hot glue pad

INSTRUCTIONS:

Cover backboard with Orange paper. • Cut moon a $4\frac{3}{4}$" circle, bats, spider, pumpkins, & headstones from cardstock. Use chalk to highlight moon & Pop Dots to attach to background. Glue on batting clouds. Hot glue tree to backboard. Build a mound around tree trunk with moss and glue in place. Add more moss and rocks along bottom of box. • Use pen to draw words on headstones and highlight with chalk. Layer pumpkins, highlight with chalk and glue together. Cut fence from Black cardstock (crosspiece is $6\frac{1}{4}$" long), glue together and highlight with White pencil. Glue fence, bats, pumpkins, & headstones in place. • **Spider**: Cut 4 wires 3" long and twist in the middle. Glue to back of one spider body. Place one end of fishing line on top of wires, cover with a Pop Dot and second body. Bend wires to form legs. Add 2 White dots for eyes. • **Spider web**: Place pattern (see diagram), under hot glue pad. On top of pad, follow lines and draw web with hot glue. Let dry. Peel off pad. Attach to glass with craft glue. Place spider at desired spot; trim filament and glue to web. Spider hangs loose. Close box and use a stencil to paint skeleton onto glass.

Pumpkins
Cut 1 each from Orange
Cut 1 each from
Yellow

Window Pane Shadowbox

by Paula Phillips

Brighten the holidays with smiles looking out from snowflake windowpanes.

SIZE: 8" x 10"

MATERIALS:
Shadowbox 8" x 10" • 3 basswood 3/8" wide strips • *Lemax* 2½" x 4" tall evergreen tree • 8" *Wrights* Red double fold quilt binding • 6 *Merry Minis* mini gift box ornaments • *Lara's Crafts* ¾" wood star • *Putnam Company* Loose synthetic snowflakes • 24" Red-White-Green rickrack • 10" White ¼" wide ribbon • 3½" x 4½" wood rectangle • 4" *Hirschberg Schutz & Co.* Silver metal chain • *Sandylion* Sticker bookplate • *ColorMates* Red paper • *Sulyn Industries* Iridescent glitter • 2 *Crown Bolt Inc.* Silver screw eyes • *Minwax* wood stain • *Folk Art* Muted Yellow acrylic paint • *Ranger* Gold Stickles glitter glue • *ColorBox* Red inkpad • *Xyron* machine • *We R Memory Keepers* Crop A Dile • Sanding block • Foam brush • Old rag or towel • Pliers • Tacky glue • Glue Dots • *3L* Tape runner

INSTRUCTIONS:
Cut basswood strips: two 10 1/8" long, and six 2 7/16" long. Sand the cut edges. Following the manufacturer's instructions, stain the basswood pieces. Let dry. • Remove the shadowbox backboard. Glue basswood onto the backboard to form the windowpanes. Glue snow in windowpane corners and sprinkle with glitter while glue is wet. Let dry. • Glue the quilt binding about the base of the Christmas tree to make a tree skirt. Paint the wooden star Yellow. Let dry. Apply Gold stickles along the outside edge of the star. Let dry. Glue star atop the tree. Using glue dots, adhere the tree and gifts in the bottom of the shadowbox. • Trim a photo to 3" x 4" and round the corners. Trim the Red paper to 3¼" x 4¼" and tape it onto the wooden rectangle. Ink the edges and sides of the wood rectangle, then sand lightly with a sanding block. Adhere photo. Punch 2 holes at the top of the wooden rectangle. Using pliers, unhook 2" of chain and attach it into one of the holes in the wooden rectangle. Repeat for the other hole. • Glue rickrack on the back side of the wooden rectangle. Let dry. Insert screw eyes into top of shadowbox to hang photo. Using pliers, attach the loose ends of the chain to the screw eyes and close the chain. • Place the sticker bookplate in the center top on the outside of the shadowbox. • Cut ribbon to fit across the corners ot the shadowbox. Run the ribbons through the *Xyron* machine to make them into stickers. Place ribbon stickers onto corners of outside of shadowbox.

1. Glue wood pieces to backboard.

2. Glue snowflakes into the corners.

Brighten Your Holidays with a Shadowbox Memento.

Play Ball

by Linda Valentino

Batter up! It's time to play ball! Here's a winning shadowbox that celebrates your love of the game.

SIZE: 8" x 10"

MATERIALS:
Shadowbox 8" x 10" • Baseball photos • Blue papers • Cardstock (White, Red, Yellow) • Vinyl 3½" baseball • 2 wood 2" baseball bats • Love ABC's • Red 1" foam stickers • Red thread and sewing machine or Red marker • Double-sided tape • Thick tacky glue • 3D foam dots

INSTRUCTIONS:
Cover backboard with papers. Tape 3 baseball cards or photos in place. Stick foam letters above cards. Cut a ¾" strip of White cardstock to fit across backing. Sew a Zigzag stitch across strip or draw with marker. Tape over seam of papers. Mat photo with Red and Yellow cardstock and adhere with 3D dots. Cut around 2 photos and adhere to matted photo using one or 2 sets of 3D dots. Tape baseball to lower right corner and glue 2 bats above ball. Let dry. Reassemble shadowbox.

Press and shape wire on the box first.

Wire Wrapped Mini Box

Shaped wire creates a pretty and easy embellishment.

MATERIALS:
Wood Box • 12" of ¼" ribbon • 28 gauge wire • Yellow acrylic paint • Mod Podge • Foam brush • Round-nose pliers • Wire cutters • *Xyron* sticker maker

INSTRUCTIONS:
Prep: Mask glass with painters tape. Paint box Yellow. Let dry.
Shape Wire: Shape wire into buds, flowers and leaves.
Assembly: Apply Mod Podge over the box and wire. Prop the lid open until dry so that it does not seal the box closed. Let dry. • Run ribbon through the sticker maker, apply ribbon to sides of the lid. Cut ribbon away from the hinges.

Wire Wrapped Mini Box

Wire Rosebuds: Wrap wire around Round-nose pliers to make a cinnamon roll shape. Use your fingers to shape the bottom of the flower bud. Cut wire. Use pliers to tuck the end under the spiral shape. Repeat for the number of rosebuds desired.
Daisy flowers: Wrap the wire to get the cinnamon roll shape as for the rosebuds. Use your fingers to bend the wire in loops around the center spiral. Cut the wire leaving about ¼". Use the Round-nose pliers to wrap the end around the loop next to it and squeeze it flat.
Leaves: Start by looping an end of the Green wire around the tip of the Round-nose pliers twice. Let the wire go straight for about ½". Make a loop and slightly pinch the end that will form the top of the leaf. Turn a smaller circle loop in the center of the leaf, then let the wire go straight again for another ½". Repeat the spirals and leaves until you have the desired length. To finish, cut the wire about ½" longer than your desired length and use the round nose pliers to make a spiral on the end.
Assembly: To flatten the shapes, place them between two sheets of paper and gently tap them flat with a hammer on a hard protected surface. • Run the wire shapes through the sticker maker and adhere to the box.

Dream Light Box

by Michele Charles

Create a dreamy night light and glowing lighted frame with gorgeous art and easy techniques.

1. Apply inks to the transparency.

2. Stamp background image.

3. Stamp image on transparency.

4. Color back of image transparency with White paint pen.

5. Layer transparencies and White paper.

6. Insert stacked transparencies and glass into box.

7. Insert the wood inner frame.

8. Insert light into box.

Create a glowing night light from a shadowbox frame.

SIZE: 5" x 7"

MATERIALS:
Shadowbox 5" x 7" • 3 sheets 5" x 7" transparency • 5" x 7" White paper • Rubber stamps (*Stampers Anonymous*, *Studio Works*) • *Tsukineko* StazOn inks (Blazing Red, Teal Blue, Mustard, Black) • Make-up sponge • *Sharpie* White paint pen • 6" portable fluorescent light • Velcro tape

INSTRUCTIONS:
Using make-up sponge, apply inks to transparency in this order: Mustard, Teal Blue, Blazing Red. Let dry. • On same side as ink colors, stamp background image in Black ink. Let dry. • Stamp "Dream" on the right-hand side of a transparency sheet. Stamp the woman image on the left side of another transparency in Black ink. Let dry. • Fill in woman and dream images on the back of the transparency with White paint pen. Let dry. • Stack the following: White paper, background transparency ink side down, "Dream" transparency , glass, and the transparcncy with the image of the woman. • Add the wood inner frame. Attach velcro to the inside frame and the light. Attach fluorescent light to inside top of frame. Reassemble shadowbox.

1. Paint the skinny trim and the edges of the wide trim Red.

2. Glue trim to the frame.

3. Paint the small wood pieces.

4. Adhere wood pieces with glue dots.

Cars Shadowbox

by Paula Phillips

Zoom, zoom, zoom! The only difference between men and boys is the price of their toys. This shadowbox features a little boy at play. This idea is a winner if used as the setting for photos of any man with his car. My brother is a mechanic and he loves this one.

SIZE: 12" x 12"

MATERIALS:
Shadowbox 12" x 12" • 1 wallet size photo • One 4" x 6" photo • Cardstock (Black, Red, White) • *Hallmark* (1 sheet "Cars" party favor stickers, 1 package of "Cars" disk launchers party favors) • Wood (car, 2 folk-art 1⅞" stars, 1½" x 2¼" sign, 4 blocks ¾" square) • *Wilton* lollipop stick • Stickers (12" sheet of narrow Black and White sticker strips, Black-White checkerboard, ½" Black letters) • Ribbon (12" White-Black dot ⅜" wide, 6" Yellow ½" wide rickrack, 9" Red gingham ¼") • 2 sticks 1" wide dentil molding • 2 sticks ½" wide decorative molding • Paint (Red, Black, White, Yellow) • Black fine tip permanent pen or marker • Paintbrush • Sandpaper • Pop dots • Glue dots (small, medium) • Wood glue • Tape runner • *Xyron* sticker maker

INSTRUCTIONS:
Cut the 1" wide dentil molding into 4 pieces: two 12⅝" and two 10⅞". Cut the ½" molding into four pieces: two 13⅝" and two 13". Sand the edges of all the molding pieces. Paint the molding as shown. Glue the trim to the frame. Let dry. • Paint the wood rectangle White. Let dry. Draw lines making 12 boxes. Paint every other square Black to form a checkerboard pattern. Let dry. Use a Black marker and outline the flag. For the flagpole, cut a lollipop stick 3" long and paint it Black. Let dry and glue it to the side of the checkerboard flag. • Paint both wooden stars Yellow. Let dry and outline the edges with a Black marker. • Paint the car as desired. Let dry. Apply stickers for the numbers on the side of the car. Adhere wood pieces to the frame. • Paint 4 wood blocks Red. Let dry. Cover the backboard with paper. Run ribbons and rickrack through the *Xyron* and adhere to backboard. • Mat photos and adhere to backboard. Apply stickers. Tie the Red gingham ribbon into 2 knots leaving 1" tails. Adhere to backboard. • On Red blocks, place a narrow sticker strip at the top and bottoms of the front side. Apply letters to spell out "C-A-R-S". Adhere blocks and disk launcher to backboard.